AF489289

Hex codes, or hexadecimal codes, are a way to represent colors in digital devices and web design. Each hex code refers to a very specific color. A hex color is expressed as a six-digit combination of numbers and letters, preceded by a pound sign or hashtag, defined by its mix of red, green, and blue (RGB). The first two letters or numbers refer to red, the next two refer to green, and the last two refer to blue.

The color values are defined as values between 00 and FF. Hex codes are a universal way to describe colors. This book is specifically about shades of blue.

A is for acid washed jeans

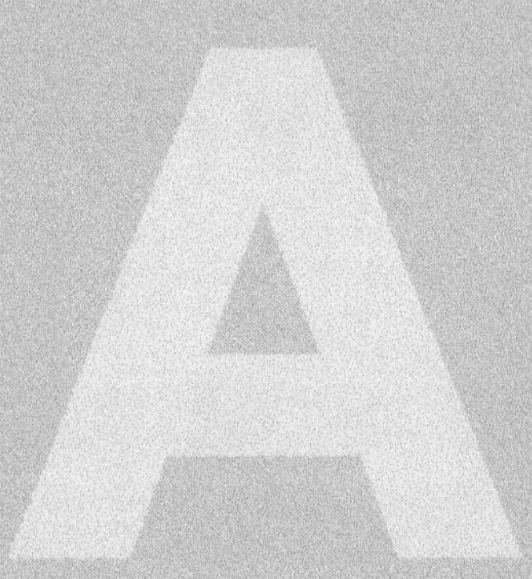

#5CB2C5

a is for agate blue

a

#75CED2

B is for b'dazzled blue

B

#2E5894

b is for bondi blue

b

\#0095B6

C is for chambray

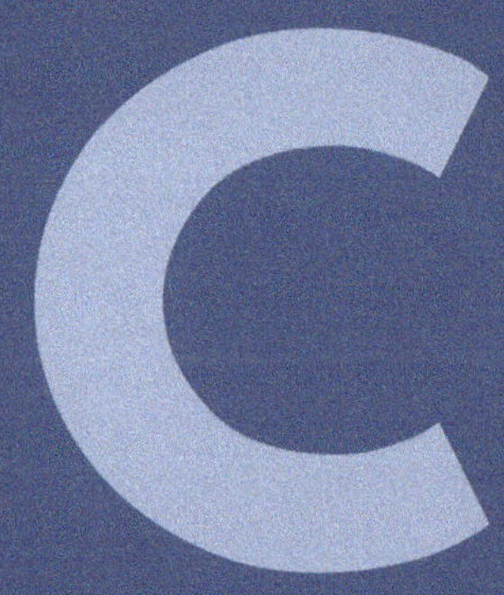

#354E8C

c is for country blue

c

#97ADD6

D is for danube

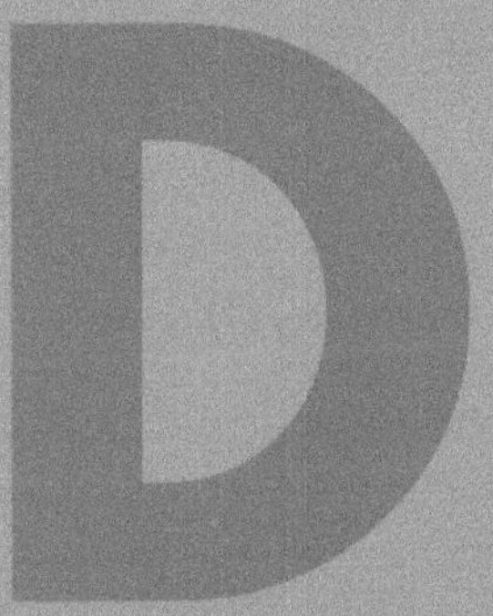

#6093D1

d is for denim

d

#1560BD

E is for endeavour

E

#0056A7

e is for endorphin

e

#4190AD

F is for foam

#D8FCFA

f is for fresh air

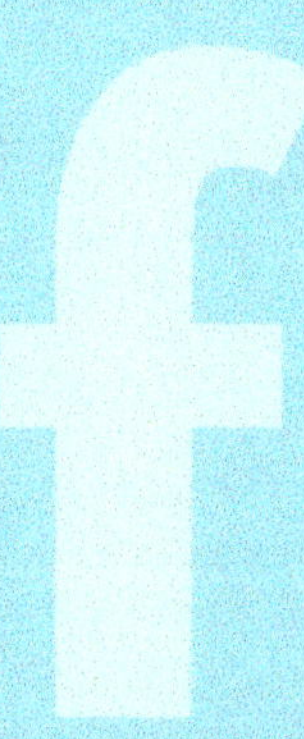

#A6E7F7

G is for glacier

#B0B3C4

g is for gulf stream

g

#80B3AE

H is for half baked blue

H

#85C4CC

h is for hullabaloo

h

#008B97

I is for ice

#B4DDF9

i is for ice cold
i
#B1F4E7

J is for jasper blue

J

#4E6590

j is for jordy blue

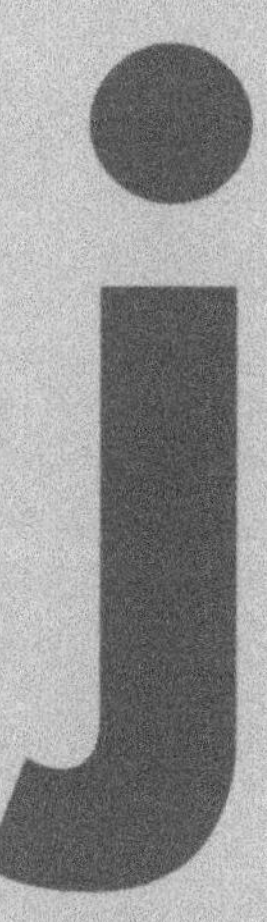

#8AB9F1

K is for kashmir blue

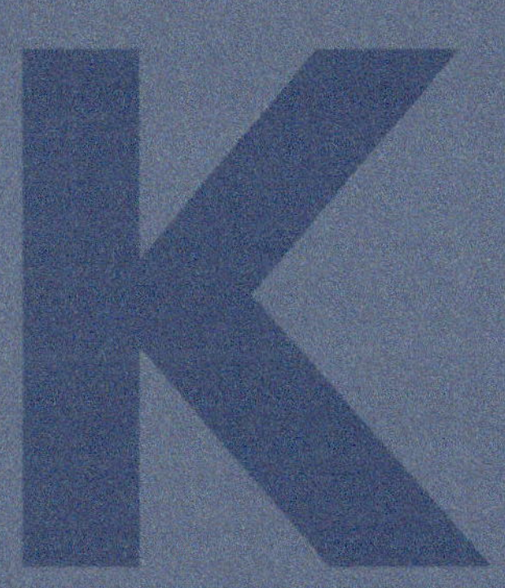

#507096

k is for kolibri blue

k

#00477A

L is for livid

L

#6699CC

I is for logido

I

#ADD4FF

M is for malibu

M

#7DC8F7

m is for mariner

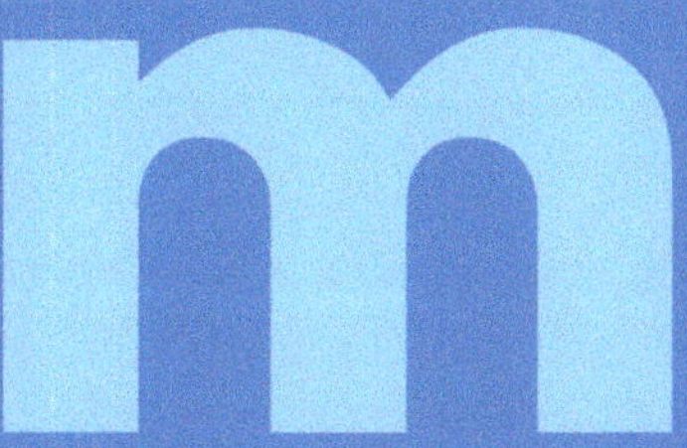

#286ACD

N is for navy blue

N

#1974D2

n is for neptune blue

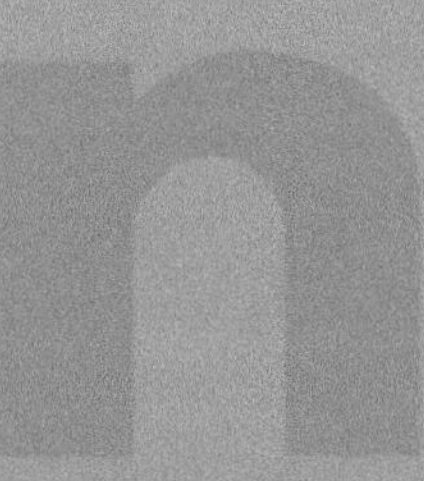

#598DE3

O is for ocean boat blue

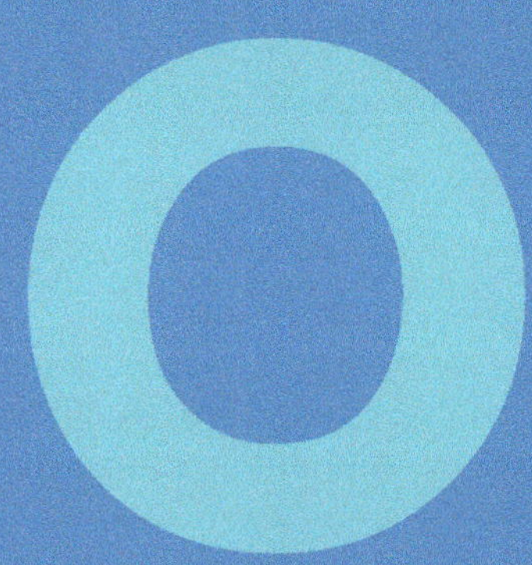

#0077BE

o is for ocean light blue

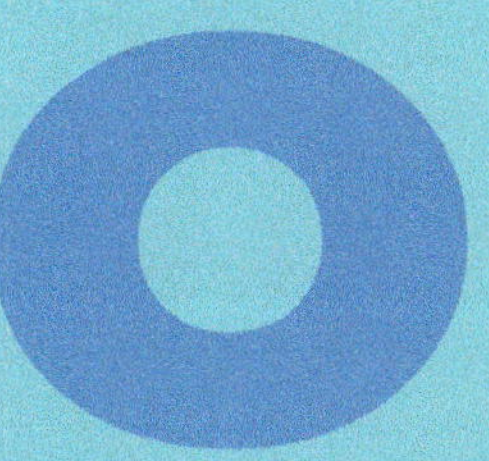

#33B5C2

P is for perano

P

#A9BEF2

p is for purwa

#9BE1FF

Q is for quark

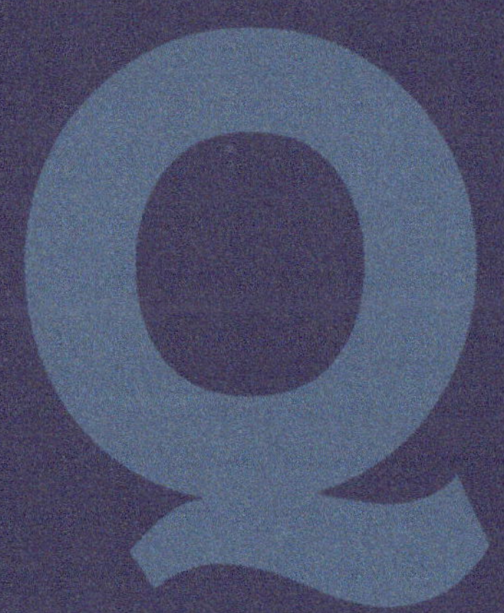

#404572

q is for queen blue

q

#436B95

R is for riptide

R

#8BE6D8

r is for robin egg blue

r

#00CCCC

S is for ship cove

S

#788BBA

s is for spray

s

#79DEEC

T is for three wishes

T

#D2DAED

t is for time out

t

#010FCC

U is for un num num num

U

#AAC2E3

u is for undersea voyage

U

#2B878F

V is for velvet blue

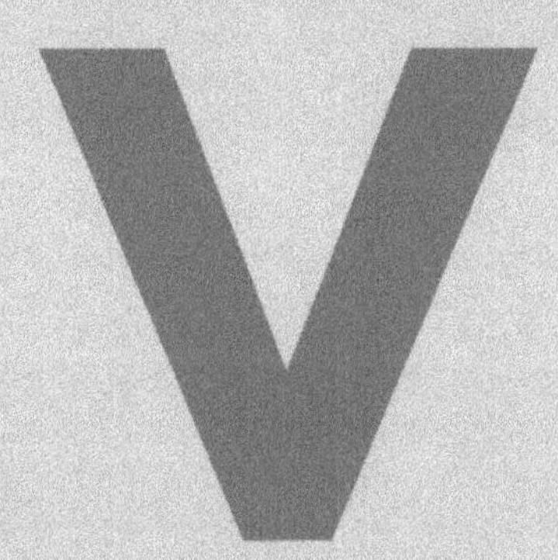

#9FCAE5

v is for vermeer blue

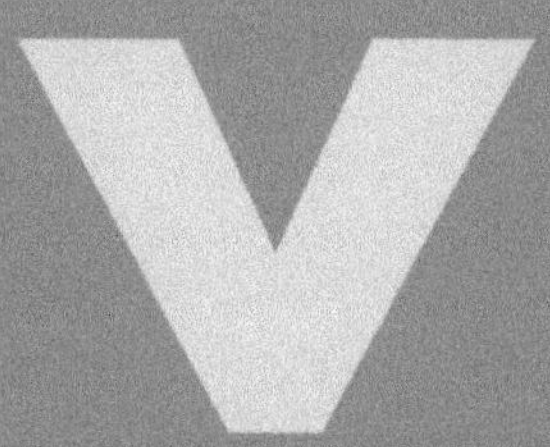

#2B7CAF

W is for warm blue

W

#6195ED

w is for waterspout

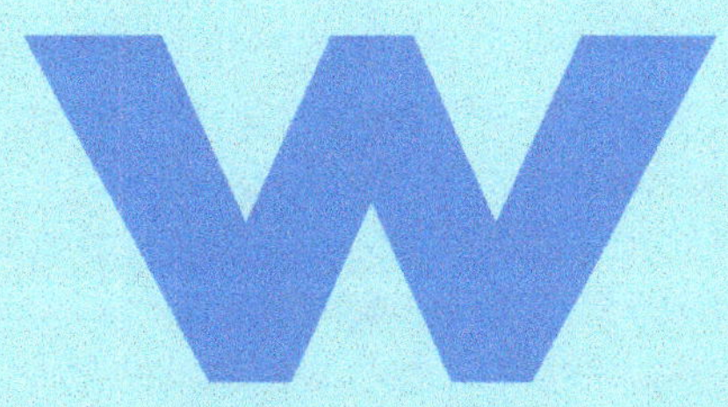

#A4F4F9

X is for xavier blue

#5FBADE

x is for xerxes blue

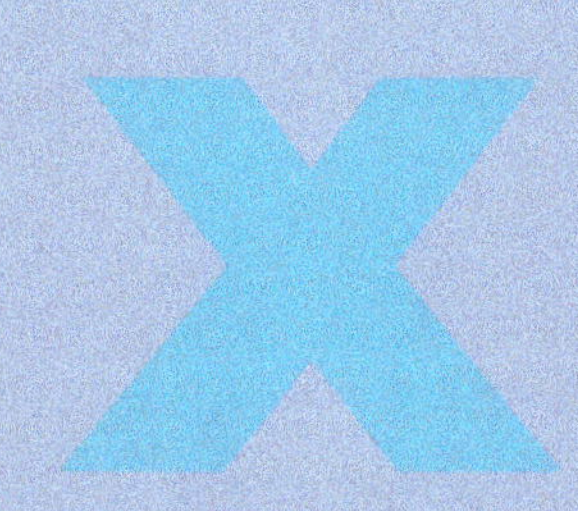

#BOCOE5

Y is for yale

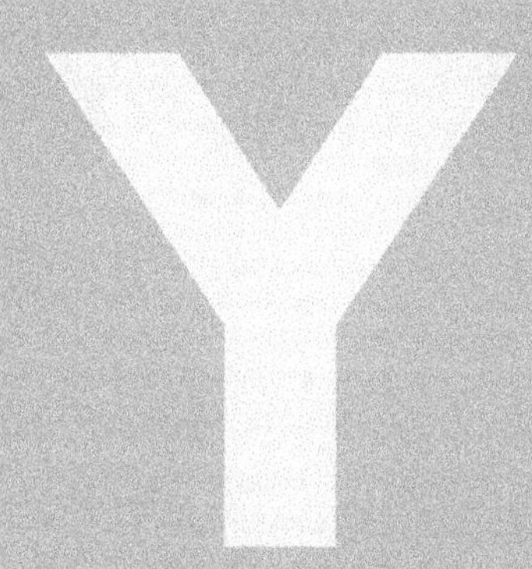

#80BBDD

y is for yearning

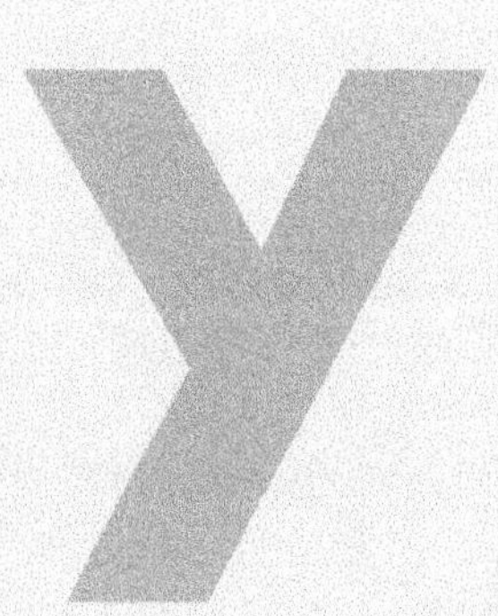

#CDE8FF

Z is for zaddick

z is for zacho blue

#9FBDD2